ST MICHAEL'S FARNBOROUGH

Hidden for a century on the Hampshire-Surrey border, the Abbey of St Michael is a little-known treasure-trove of history, faith and architecture. Crushed by exile and the loss of her husband and son, the Empress Eugénie commissioned a mausoleum and monastery at Farnborough to bury the Emperor Napoleon III and the Prince Imperial and to commend their souls to the prayers of Benedictine monks. Witness at once to the presence of God and the history of France, St Michael's remains after more than a century a place of prayer and pilgrimage.†

'You have built this church in stone, not in order to pass on to distant generations the memory of the glories of France, but because you understand that there is something greater than man's glory, more lasting than stone – the daily sacrifice of Christian prayer… This sanctuary raised on English soil will not only speak continually of the memory of the Empress Eugénie to all who come after; it will be an eloquent witness to her faith and piety.'

ABBOT CABROL AT THE FUNERAL OF THE
EMPRESS EUGÉNIE, 20 JULY 1920

The Second Empire

Charles Louis Napoleon Bonaparte was born in Paris on 20 April 1808, the son of Louis (brother of Napoleon I) and Queen Hortense de Beauharnais (daughter of Napoleon's first wife, Josephine). After the final defeat of Napoleon at Waterloo the Bonaparte family was exiled from France and had to find refuge abroad. Hortense established herself at Arenenberg in Switzerland where she lived with her son Louis.

Louis considered himself to be the official pretender to the Imperial succession and he attempted on two occasions, in 1836 and 1840, to seize power. In 1848 his moment came. Louis Philippe was forced to abdicate, the Second Republic was proclaimed and universal suffrage introduced. The Prince returned to France and was elected to the National Assembly by an overwhelming majority. By the end of that year he was also elected President of the Republic. A *coup d'état* in 1851 extended his tenure to ten years; the following year the majority of French people voted for the restoration of the Empire and so Louis Napoleon assumed the title of Napoleon III.

The Emperor married Eugénie de Guzman, Countess of Teba, of a noble Spanish family. Her father had fought for Napoleon and she herself had Bonapartist sympathies. In 1856 their only child was born – Louis, the Prince Imperial. That

ABOVE: *The Imperial family in 1857. Napoleon III looks on while Eugénie holds Prince Louis, aged just one year old, on her lap.*

RIGHT: *Monks in prayer at the lying-in-state of the Empress Eugénie, 1920. In addition to surviving relatives, the funeral was attended by King George and Queen Mary, King Alfonso of Spain, Princess Clementine of the Belgians and the ex-king of Portugal.*

same year saw the end of the Crimean War, in which France and England had fought side by side, thus consolidating the entente between the two countries for which Napoleon III worked so hard.

The Second Empire fell on 14 September 1870. Napoleon III, already suffering from the illness that was to prove fatal, had been drawn by the schemes of Bismarck into war with Prussia. The end came quickly with the disaster of Sedan. The Emperor was taken prisoner, the Prince Imperial escaped to England by way of Belgium, and the outbreak of revolution in Paris forced the Empress to flee from France to England. The three were ultimately united in exile at Chislehurst in Kent. The Emperor died there in 1873 and was buried in Chislehurst in the small Catholic church of St Mary.

ABOVE: *Louis, the Prince Imperial, in the uniform of the British Army.*

At the time of his father's death the Prince, a student at the Royal Military College at Woolwich, was preparing to take up a commission in the British army, hoping that the pursuit of a military career by a Napoleon would facilitate a possible return to France.

Anxious to take part in a campaign, he prevailed upon his mother and Queen Victoria to allow him to join the expedition against the Zulus in 1879. On 1 June, while on reconnaissance, his party was ambushed by Zulus and the Prince was surrounded and killed. He was 23 years old. Seventeen wounds from Zulu assegais, all to the front of his body, proved that he had died a brave death. To Queen Victoria and the British it was an enormous shock. To Eugénie it was the crowning tragedy. 'I died in 1879,' she would say.†

Building the Abbey

With the death of the Prince Imperial, Eugénie realized that the dynasty was unlikely ever to rule in France again and so she decided to build a mausoleum in England in their honour. The site of St Michael's in Farnborough was chosen after the landowners refused to allow the Empress to enlarge the mortuary chapel at St Mary's Church in Chislehurst, which was too small to house both imperial tombs.

Two imperial tombs required a worthy mausoleum in a worthy setting and, having considered various sites, the Empress finally decided on the purchase of an extensive property at Farnborough Hill. In the early autumn of 1881 she moved to her new home, and during the years 1883 to 1888 watched her '*basilique imperiale*' and the adjoining monastery rise on the crown of the hill opposite. The architect of the church was Gabriel Hippolyte-Alexandre Destailleur, whose only other work in this country is Waddesdon Manor, Buckinghamshire, built for Baron Ferdinand de Rothschild and erected at the same time as the imperial foundation at Farnborough.

The church is utterly French. 'France transplanted into England', wrote Monsignor Ronald Knox when writing about his reception into the Catholic Church here. Just as Waddesdon Manor is indebted to the secular architecture of the Loire region, so Farnborough consists of a number of architectural quotations from the sacred architecture of the region, particularly to the church of Notre Dame des Marais at La Ferté Bernard in the Sarthe region and to the cathedral at Tours.

The church is entered at the west end through oak doors carved in linen-fold pattern. The nave is lighted with six large windows of Flemish bottle glass, and the piers rise without interruption to blend with the vaulting.

The building combines the splendour one might expect of a royal foundation with the austerity of a monastic church. Simple, lofty arches and an Italian marble pavement draw the eye to the high altar under a richly decorated corona with the French inscription on its beams 'St Michael our glorious patron, pray for France and for England'. The Archangel's statue is above the organ. Eagles and bees – the imperial emblems – decorate the walls surrounding the High Altar.

In the north transept is the monastic choir where the monks chant daily the divine office, and in the south transept is the Queen Square altar. This altar belonged to the nuns of St Katherine's convent, Queen Square, London. The reredos, a later addition to the original altar, was added as a memorial to their chaplain, Dr Richard Littledale, author of the hymn 'Come down, O love divine' and the book *Plain Reasons Against Joining the Church of Rome*.†

LEFT: *This beautiful chair is one of a set from Toledo, donated to the monks by the Empress for use at Mass.*

RIGHT: *Gargoyles on the upper church.*

LEFT: *The view down the aisle to the High Altar. Behind the altar stands the organ, built by the celebrated Cavaillé-Coll.*

BELOW: *The Queen Square altar, given to the community by the nuns of St Katherine's Convent, Queen Square, London, to commemorate their conversion to Catholicism. They were received into the Catholic Church in 1908 by the Abbot of Farnborough.*

The Crypt

The star inlaid on the crypt floor is reminiscent of that around the tomb of Napoleon I.

Under the marble pavement of the sanctuary of the upper church lies the Imperial family, entombed in the crypt designed for that purpose. The Emperor and Prince lie in granite sarcophagi in the transepts and the Empress on a shelf high above the altar. Eugénie had chosen for herself a humble side-chapel, but 12 years before her death her place was usurped by the Queen Square altar, now in the upper church.

The crypt is a place of great irony. It has all the sobriety of a mausoleum but enjoys at the same time the warmth and intimacy of a small chapel. It is ironic that the last head of state with the name of Bonaparte should find his final rest on English soil; ironic that Louis, the Prince Imperial – the last Napoleon – should have died a British soldier and lie buried in British military uniform. There is further irony in the fact that Eugénie, to whose piety the Abbey is a memorial, lies buried dressed as a nun – a privilege of her lay association with a religious order.

The crypt is at once imperial and royal. The tombs, the gift of Queen Victoria, are an obvious echo of the tomb of Napoleon I at Les Invalides in Paris. The inlaid marble star of the floor instantly reminds one of the star around the tomb of 'our ancestor', as the young Prince used to call him. But the Prince's blood was not only imperial but also royal, since through his mother's line he enjoyed royal blood and direct descent from St Louis, King of France.

Thus the high altar of the crypt is dedicated to St Louis, and, just as the architectural features remind us of Napoleon, so they also remind us of the kings of France and the Abbey of St Denis in Paris, where a crypt in Romanesque style houses the bones of the kings of France and is crowned by the Gothic basilica that once housed the monks commissioned to pray for their souls. Few enjoy burial with the dignity enjoyed by the Imperial family at Farnborough. For more than one hundred years monks of the Benedictine Order have faithfully attended to the Empress's desire that her family should rest in a place of prayer and silence.

ABOVE: *The tomb of Louis, the Prince Imperial.*

The Empress and Abbot Cabrol, the first abbot of St Michael's, came to a compromise over the use of the crypt. They agreed that during her lifetime the crypt should be used only for Mass unless she gave express permission for other events. Soldiers in uniform should always be allowed access, she insisted, in honour of the Prince Imperial. Eugénie kept her own key to the crypt, entering through her own door half-way up the imposing Destailleur staircase. †

The Monastic Life

The monastic buildings with stone extensions added by the French monks as a copy of the mother-house at Solesmes.

St Benedict was born in Italy in about the year 480. Shocked as a student by the collapse of civilization around him, he fled to a cave at Subiaco, one hour from Rome, and led the life of a hermit. He set out for himself what he considered to be the perfect balance of human life in a rhythm of daily prayer, work and study. For prayer he took literally a line from the Book of Psalms, 'Seven times a day will I praise thee O Lord', and established seven offices or services of chanted psalms to punctuate his day. For work he prescribed crafts and manual work. For intellectual growth he recommended the study of the scriptures and the Fathers of the Church – the first centuries of Christian literature.

His way of life proved attractive and others joined him. Soon he was forced to leave Subiaco to make his first monastic foundation at Monte Cassino where his pattern of life was codified in his 'Rule for Monks', commonly known as The Rule of St Benedict. The stability and gentle order

'He is truly a monk when he lives by the work of his hands.'

FROM THE RULE OF ST BENEDICT

it established made possible a monastic life without the dramatic and excessive austerities of the ancient monks. Benedict's Rule proved enormously popular and by the end of the Middle Ages most of Europe had felt the depth of its wisdom and influence.

The Benedictine life at Farnborough was established under Abbot Fernand Michel Cabrol, Prior of the Abbey of Solesmes. Inspired by the spirit of Dom Prosper Guéranger, the founder of Solesmes, and prompted by the anti-clerical climate of France in the 1890s, Cabrol brought to Farnborough a community of monks completely dedicated to the service of God in the performance and the study of the Sacred Liturgy.

ABOVE: *The Benedictine community established by Abbot Cabrol, seated here fourth from the left. This rare photograph shows him as Prior of the community before he assumed the pectoral cross and ring as the first Abbot of Farnborough in 1903.*

RIGHT: *This beautiful book, written and illuminated at the Abbey and opened here at the Feast of St Michael, bears witness to the care and attention Benedictines have always given to the Church's worship.*

The monks increased in number with the formal exile of monks in 1903, and the original red-brick house was extended to accommodate the growing community. Numbers declined again when many of the monks returned to France for active service in the First World War. In 1922 the monks were permitted to re-establish the monastery at Solesmes and it became increasingly difficult to tempt French novices to join an abbey in Hampshire, so it was decided that the monastery should be placed under the control of English monks.

In 1947 a little band of monks came from Prinknash Abbey near Gloucester to join the remaining members of the French community and continue unbroken the monastic life here. Their own story was a fascinating one. Founded originally on Caldey Island off the Welsh coast as an attempt to form a community of monks in the Church of England, their move to Prinknash Abbey followed their conversion to the Catholic Church.†

The Community Today

Christ is not simply an historical figure but a present reality. Today men and women are still driven by Benedict's desire to 'prefer nothing to the love of Christ'. The monastery in St Benedict's Rule is therefore the 'household of God', 'the school of the Lord's service' where the monk learns to read the will of God in the scriptures, in the ancient writings of the Church Fathers, in his prayer both common and personal, in the teaching of his abbot, and the lives of his brother monks. All the monastic life is a kindling of a generous love for God, lived out in a monk's daily love for his brothers.

The life of the monks at Farnborough is influenced by the two-fold tradition of their community. From the monks of Solesmes they have inherited a love for the sacred liturgy – the solemn performance of the Prayer of the Church, and for the Gregorian Chant whose reflowering today owes so much to the Abbey of Solesmes. The Farnborough community is also part of the international Benedictine Congregation of Subiaco, a grouping of monasteries established in the last century to rediscover the ancient simplicity of the monastic life which had become clouded by the centuries.

Thus the style of life at Farnborough might be called a 'classic' or 'continental' form of monastic life, where the emphasis is on what is specific to the monastic vocation, rather than on pastoral work in school or parish, which is part of the English monastic tradition.†

Becoming a monk

After visiting and getting to know a monastery a young man might ask to become a 'postulant', living the monastic life alongside the monks. After some months he begins his formal monastic training as a 'novice', now wearing the monastic habit and being addressed as 'brother'. At the end of a year's training and a favourable report from the community, he may decide to take vows as a 'junior' monk. At least three years of further study and preparation follow before the monk may petition the community to be admitted to solemn vows. In solemn vows he promises obedience, the conversion of his life, and stability to his monastery for life. He lives and works in the monastery, and prays in the church, until finally he is buried in the monastery cemetery nearby.

LEFT: *A monk reading in the monastery's chapter house.*

'Lectio divina – The monks will devote themselves to reading.'

FROM THE RULE OF ST BENEDICT, CHAPTER 48

ABOVE: *The private prayer of each monk leads to and springs from the formal community services or 'offices' that punctuate the monastic day.*

A monk's day

5am	Rise
5.30	The Office of Vigils and private prayer
	The Office of Lauds
8.30	The Office of Terce and Mass
	Study, reading and work
12.15	The Office of Sext
12.30	Lunch
1pm	The Office of None
2.00	Work
6.00	The Office of Vespers and private prayer
7.30	Supper
8.00	Recreation
8.45	The Office of Compline and the night silence

ABOVE: *The monastery cemetery.*

'Faithfully observing the Lord's teaching in the monastery until death, we shall through patience share in the sufferings of Christ that we may deserve also to share in His kingdom.'

FROM THE PROLOGUE TO THE RULE OF ST BENEDICT

A Simple but Busy Life

In addition to the daily work of the monastery, kitchen and administration, the monks run a busy retreat house which receives many young foreign guests and monks from abroad. A printing press produces religious cards and literature and the abbey shop is kept stocked with honey, candles, and other products made by the monks of St Michael's Abbey.

What appears from the outside to be a very tranquil life can be very busy indeed, and anyone seeking escape to a monastery from the pressures of the world will just as quickly need to escape from the monastery!

Prayer, work and study within the Benedictine structure create a simple life but within an exacting timetable in which time is very precious. '*Pax inter spinas*' – peace among thorns – is a motto often used by Benedictines, symbolizing a life that is hard but which brings a deep peace within. 'Running the way of the Lord's commands,' says St Benedict, 'their hearts expand with the indescribable delight of love.' †

The cloister and monks' cells.